Brain Dead: When It Comes To Improving Mental Health, What The Hell Are We Waiting For?

Adam Smith

Published by A. Smith Media, 2022.

BRAIN DEAD: WHEN IT COMES TO IMPROVING MENTAL HEALTH, WHAT THE HELL ARE WE WAITING FOR?

First edition. December 9, 2022.

ISBN: 979-8215157381

Written by Adam Smith.

Table of Contents

To the future of mental health.

Introduction

I've finally decided to write this book about mental health. I hope it will help people who struggle with their mental health or want to strengthen their minds for a better, healthier balanced life. If we're not careful, stress can take a severe toll on our bodies.

Whether or not we're aware of it, we're all potentially contributing to a growing concern about technology overuse and its effects on mental health. We want to tell our kids to stay away from their screens and just play outside, but with every new app and game released, it gets harder for us to do so. We don't want our kids to start using their cell phones at an earlier age than we did, but for many, that's the world they've grown up in.

We are literally the epitome of a generation that is constantly connected. We are a generation of pixelated human beings. We constantly check our phones more than we brush our teeth (at least, I hope you brush your teeth).

I've caught myself mindlessly scrolling through Instagram. We spend a lot of time on our phones, but what impact does it have on our mental health?

In the chapters ahead, I'll give you some solid ways to minimize the adverse effects of stress on your health so that you can live a long, happy, and healthy life. In this book, I'll cover topics such as managing stress and coping with depression, anxiety, and other mental health issues to help you maintain a healthy lifestyle despite the pressure in your life.

You'll also learn how to create a healthy lifestyle that will help you reduce stress and improve your mental health and overall well-being. I hope you enjoy reading this book as much as I enjoyed writing it.

Chapter 1: Journal Your Gratitude and Achievements

In 2014, I began keeping a gratitude journal to write down the good things that happened every day. Gratitude doesn't just make us feel better; it makes us perform better next time. And with a journal, you can nurture gratitude and reflect on your achievements.

I needed an easy way to track my gratitude and achievements each day, along with a way to reflect on these things later. I found it easy to keep a journal, and I've already started to be more grateful and appreciate small things in my life.

I'm grateful that I can find so much to be thankful for in my life, but it's also a shame that I don't always feel like I express that gratitude as much as I should. So, to make up for it, I've been keeping a journal of things for which I am grateful, and it has helped me feel more optimistic about my life. Sometimes I'm surprised by how many things there are to be thankful for, which is nice because it reminds me that life isn't all bad, even when it feels like it sometimes.

I'm grateful to have so many wonderful friends who care about me and support me in whatever I do. It's nice to know that some people would go out of their way for you, even if they don't always agree with everything you say. I'm grateful I have a job that lets me work from home. It's nice to know that I can do whatever I want on my schedule without someone breathing down my neck telling me when to be somewhere or what tasks I need next.

I'm grateful to have a family who loves and supports me in whatever I do. It's nice to know that some people would go out of their way for you, even if they don't always agree with everything you say.

I've kept a journal since I was a child, but it's only in the last year that I've regularly written down what I'm grateful for. So much of my life was taken up by the job that I'd fallen behind in keeping track of my feelings of accomplishment.

These days, I try to write down what I'm grateful for at least once a week. It helps me stay focused on the essential things and not worry about the little things that might go wrong.

When feeling down, I like to read what I've written in my journal. It helps me remember that good things are always happening in my life and deserve recognition. I'd like to encourage everyone out there who's reading this to start a gratitude journal. You won't regret it!

Chapter 2: How to Start Your Day Right With a Cup of Coffee

Research has shown that people who have a cup of coffee in the morning have a lower rate of depression than those who don't. If you can't do coffee, try green tea instead! Coffee can be a great way to start your day. It has been proven to improve mood and mental acuity, which may help you perform better at work or school.

If you drink a cup of coffee each morning, the odds are it's doing you good. Coffee has been shown to improve sleep quality and help you wake up more refreshed. If you suffer from insomnia, try drinking a cup of coffee in the late afternoon or early evening. This will help you fall asleep faster and sleep better throughout the night.

Coffee has also been shown to improve memory and mental performance. If you're tired and groggy, try drinking a cup of coffee. It may help you think more clearly and focus better on whatever task. Coffee can also boost your mood, which may help if you're sad or depressed.

At breakfast, my wife and I share a pot of coffee. We've been doing this for over 30 years, sharing a cup of coffee every morning at breakfast. There have been many mornings during our long marriage when this daily ritual has meant a lot to us. We've shared a lot of coffee over the years. It's been a way for us to connect and talk about our day, but it's also provided a much-needed boost when we both have busy schedules. So, if you have time to enjoy your morning cup of joe, do so! Coffee can be good for you!

Imagine waking up without your morning mug of coffee. No hit of caffeine. No comforting heat from the cup in your hands. No sounds of slurping and sighs of satisfaction. Just a cold, empty room and a long day ahead. It's just not a pleasant thought. But what if you don't drink coffee? Is there another way to get your morning fix of caffeine? The answer is yes! Plenty of other drinks contain caffeine, giving you the same boost as a cup of joe. Here are a few examples:

Green tea – Both black and green tea contain caffeine, but green tea has more (about 30 mg every 8 oz). If you're looking for a healthy alternative to coffee, green tea is your best bet. It contains antioxidants and has been shown to reduce the risk of developing certain types of cancer, such as breast cancer and liver cancer. Plus, it tastes great!

Coconut water – This sweet drink is more than just refreshing: It also contains about 20 mg of caffeine per cup (8 oz). That might not sound as much as coffee or tea, but it could be enough to keep you through the day. Coconut water is also a good source of potassium, which can help lower blood pressure. And it has more fiber than any other beverage. One cup contains about 2 grams of fiber—more than an orange!Apple juice – For those who have a sweet tooth but want to avoid caffeine, apple juice might be just the thing. A cup of this delicious drink contains about 15 mg of caffeine—less than the amount in black tea and green tea but still enough to give you a boost if you need it.

Again, this is just a tiny subset of the benefits of coffee and tea. There are plenty more, but you should see that there are many reasons to start your day with a cup of joe. You'll thank me later.

Chapter 3: Plan A Getaway

For a little while every year, imagine it is already summer, and you have already booked a vacation. Write this in your calendar and start saving for it. If you're lucky enough to have a down week somewhere during the year, consider going away for that week too. That's five whole days of work free time!

There's a reason why something as simple as planning a vacation can make you happier. Having something to look forward to is an elusive key to pure happiness. Most folks make time for something fun or relaxing whenever life gets rough. Much of the time and energy we spend working could easily be spent building our little nirvana. Instead of always yearning for a future that may never take some time to plan your little getaway.

How to design a getaway:

Pick something you like to do. Go to your favorite activity and spend more than an hour there, or go to your second-favorite activity and spend more than 3 hours there. Repeat this over a few days.

Decide when you want to go and how you'll get there. Your 'time of departure' doesn't need to be the same as your 'time of arrival.' It's better if you have some flexibility with dates so that if the weather is bad when you initially plan it, you can adjust your date by a few days without starting over.

Choose when you return by adding an extra day or two to your trip based on the departure rules above. If it will take more than one day of driving each way, add a rest day, too, because after driving all day, the last thing you want to do is go all day the next day.

Choose who will be at your party based on how much room for each person in their car(s), their tolerance for hotels, etc., rather than anything else (because who are we here for?).

Choose where and when you want to show up at that new location based on what you have learned above.

Choose when to return home by adding an extra day or two to your trip based on the departure rules above.

Choose what to do when you arrive at your destination by thinking about what is available and how much time you have before it is dark.

Choose what to do during each day based on the options above (hint: if you don't get bored with them, they are probably a good choice).

Choose how to spend your time by deciding between the options above (hint: if you get bored with them, they are probably not a good choice).

Choose how to get from place to place by thinking about what is available and how much time you have before it is dark.

Choose where to eat based on the options above (hint: if they taste good, they are probably a good choice).

Choose what to do when you leave your destination by thinking about what is available and how much time you have before your plane leaves or you need to check out.

Whether traveling alone or with friends, we are setting up a true getaway is crucial to a successful vacation. This is the most effective way to look forward to something, as we all know. Regarding how long that happiness boost will last, anywhere from 4 to 8 days is typical, depending on the person and how exciting their trip was.

There is also evidence that suggests regularly taking vacations can increase overall happiness and help prevent depression and anxiety. So take this study as an opportunity to plan a getaway for the next time you need a mental break!

Chapter 4: Work To Your Strengths

Want to be more productive? Have more energy and enthusiasm? Maybe you'll find some inspiration from these stories of people who have found success with their strengths.

When faced with a challenging task, it's easy to get stressed and worry. We might even say things like "I can't do this" or "I'm not good enough to handle this." The funny thing is, when we do this, we usually talk about something a lot easier for us (and something we are good at). That's because we're trying to build up from where we are (where it's easy). I want to show you how you can use your strengths to help you get better at something.

When we feel good about what we're doing, it shows. Studies show that we perform better when we feel good about our skills. And with the uncertainty of a new career looming, we don't want to let ourselves or anyone else down.

Try this one. Do you know the saying "Work your strengths, not your weaknesses."? It's great in theory, but it can be hard to do. I mean, let's say you're a terrible public speaker. Get up in front of the room and try to give a speech. Not fun! But tackling those more challenging tasks will be easier if you work on your strengths first. Let's say you're great at programming computers. Start by learning a new programming language, then move on to giving a speech about it.

You'll feel more comfortable and confident with computers, making it less scary when it comes time for that public speaking test in class (if you decide to take that route).

The next time you set out to do something, start with something you're good at. It'll build your confidence, give you a sense of accomplishment, and make it easier for you to tackle something more challenging.

You've got the basics down. You know what you're doing and can do it without thinking about it. Now it's time to make your life easier by working on a task that gives you a bigger bang for the buck.

I think you should be proud of yourself for trying to learn something difficult. So take a few minutes to pat yourself on the back, then give this another try. I bet you'll do better.

When writing, you must get in your way. Your internal editor will stop you from writing. Work on one aspect of your paper and once you master it, move on to the next.

The next time you're feeling down about your past failures, remember this: every successful person has had failures. They're just like you. They've learned from them, moved on, and achieved success. The difference is they didn't let their losses hold them back in the future. They didn't give up when things got tough, or people told them no. They kept going. They learned from their mistakes and didn't stop until they achieved success.

The difference is they took action, even if it was small. They kept going when others would have quit. They kept going. You can do the same.

I was pretty good at this but lacked the self-confidence to go further. I was stuck in a rut, unable to move forward. I didn't want to be the failure everyone thought I would be. So I got help from a therapist who helped me identify my limiting beliefs and how they held me back.

I learned it was okay to be imperfect and make mistakes. I realized that failure is just a stepping stone to success. No one is perfect, but we can learn from our mistakes and confidently move forward.

I realized my mistakes were a part of who I was, not something to be ashamed of. I didn't have to hide or try to cover them up with excuses and lies. Instead, I could own up to my shortcomings and move on.

I learned to embrace my imperfections because I learned it is okay to be imperfect and make mistakes. I realized failure is just a stepping stone on the path to success. No one is perfect, but we can learn from our mistakes and confidently move forward. I didn't have to hide my shortcomings or try to cover them up with excuses and lies. Instead, I could own up to what happened and move on without fear of being judged or ridiculed by others.

I'm not the kind of person who's good at everything. I can't do math, don't understand science, and am a lousy artist. But I have one almost unrivaled skill: I can edit anything – a book, an article, or a speech – and improve it.

The next time you find yourself at a loss, looking for a way to break out of a slump, try doing something you're good at. If you're unclear about your strengths, pay attention to the moments when you feel calm and in control; the chances are that your muscles will be on display. Once you've found something that suits you, tackle a more significant task that incorporates just one of these strengths; this will help reinforce your understanding of what works best for you.

Remember, everything takes time, and you can't do everything. But it's possible to get better at just about anything with a little effort and willingness to try new things. The same approach is accurate for any creative pursuit: writing, painting, drawing. Start by trying something you love, then work your way up to new challenges as motivation and skills improve. The greatest creators didn't achieve greatness by mastering some skill overnight, so don't expect yourself to do the same.

Chapter 5: Sleep Better With Cooler Temperature

Did you know that your bedroom, where you sleep, should be kept at a temperature between 60 and 67 degrees Fahrenheit? Research has shown that optimal sleep temperature is key to a good night's sleep. Keeping the temperature in your room too hot or cold can disrupt sleep. It could even lead to poor mental health, affecting your daily job performance. So, what's the optimum temperature for sleep?

The optimal temperature for sleep is 60-67 degrees Fahrenheit. Your body temperature naturally drops a few degrees when you are ready for sleep, and to fall asleep, your body temperature needs to drop even lower. To achieve this, it's essential to let it adjust to the ambient temperature of your bedroom. A higher-than-normal room temperature will prevent your body from adapting to the right level.

Everyone deserves fantastic sleep, but it's not always as easy as it sounds. With the rise of technology, distractions and disruptions at night are commonplace. According tosleepfoundation.org, 35% of adults between 18 and 64 will use their smartphones, tablets, or laptops while they are in bed. That statistic is roughly 30% higher than just a few years ago. It's easy to see why we don't get enough sleep and why good sleep has become somewhat of an elitist club.

But the good news is that there are plenty of ways to improve your sleep quality and quantity.

It's crucial to me that you keep your bedroom at a comfortable temperature for sleeping. I know it's not easy, especially if you're a person who tends to run hot (like me).

It's why the air conditioner in my bedroom is always set to 66 degrees. I've learned that my body is happier when it's not too hot or cold. And I know that if I have trouble sleeping, it's because of my room's temperature.

So, try adjusting the temperature if you've tried everything else and still aren't sleeping well. Even just a few degrees can make a big difference.

If you decide to change the temperature in your room, try to keep a consistent schedule—one that you can comfortably stick to and won't be interrupted by changes in the weather or other factors—both for sleeping and waking up. Just remember: if you decide to adjust your thermostat, consider the natural fluctuations of your local climate. That way, you'll be able to get a better night's sleep no matter what the forecast calls for.

There is no one-size-fits-all strategy when it comes to sleep – although some key strategies can be used as a general guide in most cases. The first step is to experiment and see if you can figure out what works for you. Putting these strategies into action could help improve your sleeping patterns – and, consequently, your mental health.

The best advice we can give you is to take care of your health. There are plenty of ways to do this, from keeping yourself active to eating a balanced diet, among other things. Remember that sleeping is an essential part of your health and well-being, so go to sleep and wake up reasonably every day. Your body and mind will thank you!

Chapter 6: The Mental Approach To Finding The Good Life

Improve your mental health by figuring out what's making you unhappy or stressed and doing something about it.

You may ask yourself, how on earth can I improve my mental health? Well, the first thing you should try to improve is your mindset. A person's mindset is how they look at things and think about them. If you train your mind to think more positively, you will be closer to improving your mental health.

A simple trick to accomplish anything in life is to make a plan, do the first thing, and then the next. The only difference is you can't lose weight overnight. You need to take it step by step and be diligent about getting started. Start today, and don't forget to focus on yourself.

Make a list of things you need to change, but don't try to decide which one to do first. No matter how good things are, there is always room for improvement.

Nobody can control other people, but we can indirectly influence some aspects of our surroundings and interpersonal relationships. First and foremost, we can control ourselves and our actions. We can take action to change what is happening inside us, as well as to affect our surroundings.

Though it's easy to become immobilized by the demands of life, you can take small steps to improve your life and get yourself off your butt.

Let's face it: having a clear picture of your life and where you are going is important.

A few weeks ago, I had the pleasure of attending a conference on happiness. It was veritable who's who of the happiness movement, and I took many notes on the discussed strategies and tactics.

One of the things that were repeated ad nauseam was the importance of vision. The more clearly you can see where you want to go, the more motivated you will be to get there. But a vision alone is not enough; it must be coupled with action steps toward achieving that goal.

The problem with most visions is that they are too vague. They don't have enough detail to be useful. You could say that a vision is like a map, but it's not good if you can't read it!

But it's not just a matter of being able to read the map; you also have to be able to draw one. And this is where most people fall short. They don't know how to go from idea to action, so they never get anywhere.

The best way to create a vision is to write it down. Then you'll have something concrete to work with and refer back to when you need inspiration. You can also use a vision board, which is literally a board with pictures that represent what you want in your life.

We all have areas we'd like to improve: better health, relationships, greater productivity, and so on. But if you're not making progress, it's easy to grow discouraged and give up altogether – but it doesn't have to be that way. After all, we are at different places in life – some with more time than others.

Life is a book, and how you read it changes its story. How you choose to see things, interpret them, and react will ultimately make all the difference in how you experience your life, respond to the world around you, and how others perceive you.

Chapter 7: Always Be Testing

Or "experimenting" is a better term. It can be hard to tell why when we're happy because creativity flows from so many sources. This is a great time to immerse yourself in art and as you do, be sure to take notes on your feelings. You may start painting or writing, but you will eventually want to apply the creative process in some practical way that leads you toward a more satisfying life.

Did you know that psychologists agree that creativity is very important to overall mental health? Studies have shown that people who spend a little time doing something creative each day tend to experience less stress, anxiety, and depression, often leading to a more positive outlook on life.

When you're in a good mood, try thinking about what you have to be grateful for. Make a list of all the things that are going great in your life, whether it's family, health, friends, or career. You'll feel happier and more optimistic by writing down the things you're grateful for.

Taking time out of your day to focus on self-care can bring so much pleasure into your life, and you may also be surprised at how great it is for your mental health. I know that in my own life, daily mindfulness practice has improved my overall mental health. I'd love to hear about your favorite healthy habits in the comments.

Can you feel a difference when you're not being creative? Of course, you can! Creativity is fundamental to our mental health and happiness. We're more comfortable, socially and emotionally resilient, and experience less depression. And, get this: we experience less anxiety too!

There isn't one path to happiness or well-being. What works for one person may not work for another.

I found this out when I tried my hand at a new craft. It felt so good to have made something I wanted to use as an opportunity to try out some other projects.

I am so glad that I did! I found that I had a lot of fun making things. It was also very relaxing and meditative.

I don't know about you, but the creative projects I undertake are usually restricted by my imagination and not a lack of time.

If you are stressed out and want to try something new, consider picking up a hobby. Maybe it's just writing in a journal or painting with watercolors. Or perhaps you like to cook and could use the opportunity to bake some cookies or make some homemade pasta sauce.

There are so many possibilities! Don't be afraid to fail. I hope that you find something new to enjoy. I think the most important thing is finding something you love doing. If you don't, you will find it hard to feel like you are making progress. Maybe writing in a journal isn't your thing, but perhaps painting with watercolors is! The point is that there is no right or wrong way to do something (unless they are illegal, of course).

Chapter 8: Show Some Love

Are you crushing on someone? Do you love your best friend? Is your family awesome? If you answered yes to any of these questions, I suggest showing someone some love!

Who on earth doesn't want to be happy and healthy? And it's not just me saying this. Experts in psychology and psychiatry all agree that strong, close relationships are vital to happiness and good health. Can you think of anything else that can make such a difference? I can't. Of course, building and maintaining relationships isn't accessible, nor is it always simple. But those are things I like to focus on.

Everyone has someone who means a lot to them: a sister, brother, parent, spouse, child, sweetheart, or friend. But have you noticed how much better you feel when in love? I mean really in love — not just infatuation. Sure there's that exhilaration and the butterflies in your stomach when the object of your affection walks into the room. But those aren't the things that make your heart flutter. That more profound feeling comes when you look into their eyes and know they're the one for you.

I don't know about you, but I spend a lot of time working. Between writing, reading and editing content, and consulting for several other businesses (not to mention running my companies), I was working more than 40 hours a week — not that I mind all the work. Still, one of the things that suffer is healthy personal relationships. My dad once told me, "You can't pour from an empty cup." True enough, you can't be a giver if you aren't also a receiver — of love, care, support — whatever it may be.

So I decided to do something about it. To make time for myself and my relationships with loved ones. I started by cutting down on social media, reading fewer books (this one included), and spending less time on the internet — in short, by unplugging from my devices.

Tell someone that you appreciate them and why. Maybe it's a family member or a friend. Send a card, a text, or call them to show your love.

Remember to say "I love you" to someone in your life. If you're too shy, send them an email instead (tell them I said they should accept your email as a love letter).

No matter where you are, who you are with, or what you are doing, show someone you care about them. I challenge you to express your appreciation for someone in your life. If you are having a hard time coming up with someone, try thinking of the people who have had the most positive impact on your life.

We must take time out of our busy schedules to spend time with the people we love. We must tell the people in our lives that we care about them. It may seem like a small act, but it can make a big difference in someone's day.

If you're having difficulty coming up with someone to express your appreciation for, try thinking of the people who have had the most positive impact on your life. We must take time out of our busy schedules to spend time with the people we love. We must tell the people in our lives that we care about them. It may seem like a small act, but it can make a big difference in someone's day.

Share some love with your friends, family, and even a stranger today. You can make someone's day by simply letting them know you care about them.

Ultimately, you need to reach out and connect with others. Find that inner strength and be the best version of yourself by encouraging others to do the same. A strong support structure is a key to a happier life.

Be sure to share these tips with your friends. Being there for each other and having that support network of close relationships is essential to a happy, healthy life. It's not always easy to find the words or the time, but it's important to remember that words are mighty powerful. And one of the best things you can give someone is your time and support.

Whether a person needs help, is unaware that he or she needs help, or is unwilling to seek help for mental health concerns, the best thing we can do as loved ones is to be supportive and available when needed. There's nothing wrong in trying to improve someone else's mental health—it takes a lot of hard work and determination, but it can happen if they are willing.

It's important to remember that when someone loses a fundamental relationship (e.g., a friend or family member), they will need support from others as they cope. And although we're not professional counselors or psychologists, experiencing loss—whether it be a breakup, a move, the death of an important loved one, etc.—can have huge effects on our mental health and well-being. So next time you hear about the loss of a friend or loved one, don't hesitate to reach out and lend an ear so they may share their feelings.

Have you noticed that most depressed people are rarely alone? And the happiest people are constantly surrounded by friends and loved ones. You can learn from this that keeping yourself open to friendships and relationships is imperative. You need these bonds to be a happy, healthy person. The trick is to stay positive, even in a non-ideal situation. For example, therê may be an annoying co-worker who bothers you every day – understand why they're acting like this, even if it's the wrong reason, and fix the problem if possible.

Chapter 9: Increase Energy With Chocolate, No Kidding

Researchers concluded that dark chocolate "enhances mood and brain function and may be an effective cognitive enhancer" due to its flavonoids, caffeine, and theobromine content. It can also improve your focus – not only while eating chocolate but even after it's digested! Most of the studies were conducted on healthy adults and young students, so more research is needed to determine how Theobromine affects a teenager's brain or a person with a mental illness.

Why not just eat chocolate every day? I'm sure you've heard the rumor that chocolate is bad for you. It has been said that chocolate can increase blood pressure. This "chocolate myth" is long gone. We now know that chocolate improves blood pressure and benefits our heart health.

Remember the cost of healthy brain power. It's worth it because, without your brain, you would perish. If you want some serious results when it comes to mental health, you have to take it seriously and make a few lifestyle changes.

Everyone loves to indulge once in a while, or at least I would hope so. Whether you're having a pb&j sandwich or ice cream or washing it down with some root beer, there is nothing quite like that feeling of satisfaction after indulging. Sometimes (if we're not careful), we don't wait to indulge, though, and sometimes those indulgences are just a bit too rich and leave us wanting to run to the bathroom. If you have ever felt this way, you should try eating dark chocolate regularly as part of a healthy diet plan.

Can you improve your mental health by eating better? All mental health disorders are caused by something. And while some people believe that they can be blamed on a vitamin deficiency, the truth is that most psychological issues are either the result of, or exacerbated by, diet.

Feed your brain!

Treat yourself to a couple of pieces of dark chocolate every few days. The flavonoids, caffeine, and theobromine in chocolate are thought to work together to improve alertness and mental skills.

Next time you need a mental energy boost, don't reach for an energy drink or an apple. Reach for a couple of pieces of dark chocolate instead.

Chocolate's also good to keep around when you're in the middle of a project that is making you crazy. A little nibble can boost your brainpower and make it easier for you to stay focused on the task.

Next time you feel sleepy, skip the coffee and grab a square or two of dark chocolate instead.

You can also get the same effects from caffeine and other compounds found in chocolate.

I now have a new way to enjoy chocolate – as a pick-me-up for my brain and body.

Now it's time to take action and enjoy the slight boost in brainpower you'll have in just a few minutes.

I'm not a big chocolate easter, but I could easily make an exception for one of these decadent desserts.

I remember when I was in school, and we'd have a pop quiz, and I was so busy at work that I couldn't go to the library to study. So, I set up a "mini-library" in my bedroom.

I pulled out all my textbooks and set them up on the dresser and desk. Then I found some of my notes from class, ripped them into pieces, and taped them to the walls. It was like my own little study hall!

I didn't do this every day, just when I was swamped and needed to cram for a test. It helped me remember everything I'd learned in class that week and made studying less boring!

Many people use this technique to help them remember things like where they parked their cars. When you get ready to leave the mall, for example, take a few minutes before you go out and walk around the parking lot looking at all the cars. Then write down keywords or phrases that describe your vehicle so you can easily remember which one is yours when you're driving home later.

Okay, now back to the chocolate thing.

Have you ever heard of an association called the International Society for Neurofeedback and Research? No, me neither. But apparently, they also like dark chocolate because they showed that this indulgence is not harmful but not good for you. So it seems that a couple of pieces, about 10g daily, are fine for you.

As we mentioned earlier in the chapter, most people crave sugar when they're experiencing a bout of depression—but that doesn't make refined sugar the solution. Refined sugar could be making your problems worse. Instead of reaching for processed sweets, try eating some dark chocolate instead. It's one of the healthier choices and can immediately make you feel better. If you aren't someone who eats chocolate all that often, dark chocolate is an indulgence you can feel better about—natural sugars combined with cocoa (or cacao) powder create a sweet treat that's much safer than your typical bar of Ben & Jerry's.

And while you're at it, consider the numerous other benefits of dark chocolate, including "skin health and collagen production" and the ability to "increase blood flow." Also, if your memory is falling a little short, grab some walnuts—they've been shown to help improve memory. Finally, make it a rule to get outside for at least 20 minutes daily to increase Vitamin D levels and benefit from exercise. It might just be enough to turn your frown upside down.

Food can have a powerful impact on your overall brain health and your mental attitude. Whether you're starting to feel the winter blues or just want to improve your ability to concentrate, these simple steps are easy to incorporate into your daily routine. More than that, they might just be the key ingredients for taking your mental health to a new level.

While there is much information about nutrition and supplements on the web, it's not always the factor we need to focus on. We think that if more people can take it upon themselves to take care of their mental health and fix those weak points in their life, they will inevitably have a happier experience through the ups and downs that life brings us all.

Chapter 10: The Agony Within

Many people experience at least one traumatic event that causes mental damage. You can only heal what you feel and allow yourself to handle it, so writing a journal is the best way to deal with your ordeal. This writing will let you calm down, reflect on your feelings and see the truth. The author's journal entries are the leading example of this.

Most people do not realize that mental health is as important as physical health. Mental health issues cause just as many problems in other countries as in America. I am focused on the causes of such disorders and how we can deal with them to make society better in the future.

It takes a lot of courage and self-control to keep living while holding on to all the painful and traumatic experiences in our lives. Wouldn't it be great if there were good people around us to help eliminate all these unwanted feelings and lead healthier, happy, more meaningful, and creative lives?

It's a trick I learned from my mother. When someone does you wrong, it's easy to bear a grudge. But if you hold onto it for too long, you'll end up poisoning your heart.

Unresolved trauma tends to pass from one generation to the next. Our children can avoid it if we can reach out and provide counseling and therapy so that they understand their issues or learn healthy ways of dealing with them.

An estimated 26.2 percent of American adults suffer from a diagnosable mental disorder in a year. This translates to nearly half of all Americans at any given time and over 50 percent of those surveyed in any given month. With this data, it seems that mental illness is a significant part of our lives, and if we are not suffering from it, we are someone's caretaker, family member, or friend.

The statistics show that a large percentage of the population is mentally ill, and it is essential to understand what this means. Mental illness is a term that covers a wide range of conditions, including depression, anxiety disorders, eating disorders, schizophrenia and personality disorders.

While there are many differences between the conditions, they all have one thing in common: they affect the mental health of their sufferers. The symptoms of mental illness vary widely from person to person and can include changes in sleeping patterns, eating habits, activity levels, or self-perception.

Mental illness can significantly impact your daily life, leaving you isolated and alone. It may be challenging to understand what someone with mental illness is going through if you have never experienced it. However, these statistics show that many people worldwide suffer from some kind of mental health problem.

The good news is that there are ways you can help. Mental health support groups, counseling, and therapy are all services that can be accessed by anyone who feels they need extra help dealing with their condition.

These services are free and confidential, which is an excellent option for those who want help but don't have the money to pay for it. If you think someone you know might be suffering from mental illness, don't be afraid to ask them how they are feeling.

You never know whether they might open up to you and let you help them out. If you are concerned about your mental health, don't be afraid to seek support from friends and family or a healthcare professional.

You can also contact a support group or the National Suicide Prevention Lifeline at 1-800-273-TALK (8255).

It is important to remember that mental illness is treatable, and many people are willing to help you. Don't give up hope if you are suffering from a mental health condition.

Don't keep anger inside long. Anger suppressed and not expressed can poison the person who holds it.

They become toxic if anger, frustration, and resentment are not expressed.

This is the best solution for you to get rid of your anger. If you keep your anger inside for a long time, it will hurt your health. Even if you think the person you are angry with doesn't deserve to suffer, the longer you hold on to the anger, the worse it makes you feel.

It's not easy to bottle up your feelings because when you do, it's like a pressure cooker – one of those where the lid has a little venting on it so that if something gets too hot inside, some steam can escape.

The advice to "Don't keep anger inside long" is widely attributed to the Dalai Lama. Some variations include "Don't let anger build up inside, or it will make you sick."

It is true that if you hold onto your feelings, they can become toxic. The longer you keep anger inside, the worse it makes you feel. If you want to let go of the hurt or frustration, for example, write down what happened and how it made you feel.

Then, put the paper aside and don't read it for a few days. You may be surprised by what you find. If you are holding onto anger or resentment, try writing down what happened and how it made you feel. Then, put the paper aside and don't read it for a few days – or weeks if possible.

You may be surprised by what you find. If you are holding onto anger or resentment, try writing down what happened and how it made you feel. Then, put the paper aside and don't read it for a few days – or weeks if possible.

Keeping anger in can be costly and dangerous. Don't wait until everything is lost and you want to explode, so take a deep breath and let that hatred go.

Forgiveness is one of the most challenging concepts to wrap our heads around. It's easy to say, "be forgiving" or "forgive those who have wronged you," but it's another thing to act on that hope. We all have our limits, and while we think forgiveness is a virtue, sometimes it doesn't come naturally.

It's important to remember that you have the power to decide how you react to external circumstances. You are in control of your inner posture, and no matter what kind of day you're having, you can choose to look on the bright side. Seek out positive opportunities to share yourself with others and radiate the love around you. Take solace in the happy moments that life brings, breathe deeply and freely, and remind yourself that all will be well with time—no matter how things might seem at present.

If you're feeling frustrated with someone else, take a moment to consider how you might feel if they were in the same situation. For example, if your partner is late for dinner again and didn't call to let you know, try imagining how this would affect your day and what it would mean if he or she suddenly stopped showing up. Would it be okay? How would that make you feel? We often assume that other people's actions are meant to hurt us or complete our lives harder than they have to be—but we have no idea what's happening inside someone else's mind.

It's easy to think that someone else's behavior is intentional or malicious when, in fact, it might be completely unintentional. Try to find some compassion for the person who has wronged you—you may be surprised by how much this changes your perspective.

Chapter 11: Sometimes Less Is More

Sometimes, you already do many fun things and are still unhappy. This can be frustrating, especially when your goal is to add more fun to your life. So what else can you do to make yourself more comfortable? It turns out that sometimes we need to stop adding new activities to get more pleasure.

Instead, it can be more effective to cut out some things that make you unhappy. In other words, it's not just about adding more fun activities but also cutting back on the things that drain your energy and make you feel bad about yourself.

After reading a fascinating discussion on Reddit, in which one respondent pointed out that their life lacked "emotional depth," I started wondering what would bring more depth and pleasure to my own life. What activities could I add or subtract from my life to improve it? No one involved in improving mental health can decide what will work for your specific life. But there are many different ways you can improve your mental health and, I hope, your happiness along the way.

I've been thinking about this question for a while, and I don't have any answers. But I want to say that if you can find a way to make your life more emotionally complex and exciting, it will probably improve your mental health.

So the obvious question is, why don't we just add more activities to our life to make it more pleasurable?

I don't think we need to add new activities to make life more pleasurable. It's all about changing your attitude toward the things you already do.

Maybe it's not a good idea to try and "add" new activities. Instead, perhaps we can shift how we perceive and experience our daily pleasures.

I have some suggestions that might help you get more pleasure from what you're already doing.

I used to think I could only enjoy things more if I added new activities. But the more I've thought about it, the more I've realized that I can enjoy things just as much again by doing them better.

You might even be able to do some of the things you love with less effort and more fun! It's simple. You'll love getting things done with less effort and more enjoyment.

The ideas you can apply to your life will help make you happier, healthier, and more effective.

By making more intelligent, conscious choices, you'll be able to spend less time, money, and effort getting the desired results. It's much easier than you think! All the materials for this simple technique are readily available and safe.

The first step is to assess your current state and determine the areas burdening you. Then you can start setting up a game plan to make things easier and fun!

But you can also extol the virtues of what's already in your life – like a good book, a nice cup of tea, or a walk in the park – and improve your time.

A few years ago, as part of an experiment that I'm still running, I started keeping track of all the different activities I do each day.

I do this by writing down what I did and the time spent in my notebook. This way, I can see how many hours I spend on different things and which activities are more or less productive. I also track how much fun each exercise is for me – because that's important too!

I keep track of all this because I want to know what makes me happy and when. If I don't know what makes me happy, then it's hard to decide how much time and energy I should spend on a particular activity. For example, some people think watching TV is relaxing; for me, it's not because it doesn't make me feel good after doing it.

So, I try to track what makes me happy and when. This helps me decide how much time and energy I should spend on different activities.

I also try to ensure that my life is full of things that make me happy. I don't mean that I want to do only fun things, but rather that I want my life to be full of many different activities, some of which are fun and some not so much. For example, the other day, I went out with a friend and had lunch at a Tex-Mex restaurant.

It was a lot of fun, but it wasn't fun because we ate nachos and talked about our lives. Instead, I was happy about the lunch because I got to spend time with an old friend.

I know that sounds like a straightforward thing, but it's true. Spending time with someone you care about is one of the best things in life, and it doesn't have to be all fun, either. Sometimes when I'm hanging out with friends and have nothing planned, we'll just walk around or watch a movie together. Those are some of my favorite times because they're not particularly exciting, but they're still fun.

We do that with things we need – food, shelter, clothing. But sometimes, we forget to add new positive activities to our lives to make them more vibrant. Take time to keep taking care of your happiness and the things you genuinely enjoy doing.

There are, after all, ways to improve your mental health and keep yourself feeling good whether you're out on the town or at home, enjoying an evening in. It simply comes down to knowing what can give you pleasure and taking action to feel those benefits. Whether mental or physical, a little bit of pleasure can improve your overall mood and outlook and your health.

Take time to do something you enjoy with people you love. These activities might be ones you usually participate in or even ones new to you. If extra resources are available, a class or seminar in one of these areas may be worth considering. I'm sure it will be a welcome pace change and a nice break from your typical routine.

Chapter 12: Take A Trip Down Memory Lane

Some of us find it relaxing to take a trip down memory lane to build new happy memories. But, for those dealing with anxiety, that isn't always possible.

When we're having a bad day, it's hard to reflect on the good times. Instead, our minds are filled with all the terrible things that have happened in our lives—and what might happen. We can't help but focus on the negative and worry about everything that could go wrong.

The more we focus on negative thoughts, the more anxious we feel. The more anxious we feel, the harder it is to think positively or have any sense of enjoyment in life.

But we don't have to let anxiety rule our lives. There are ways we can use it as an opportunity to make positive changes in ourselves and our lives. When we're sad or anxious, we can focus on what's going right instead of what's going wrong. We can take time for ourselves and do things that make us happy.

We can focus on what we're grateful for instead of what's missing from our lives. And we can try to feel better by taking action and doing something positive for ourselves or somebody else.

Life can be pretty stressful, can't it? We don't always have time to do the things we want, and so many challenges and obstacles come our way daily. One of the best ways to improve our mental health is by taking time out of our day to take up a hobby or pastime. Coloring is an excellent option when you're feeling stressed, anxious, or just want to enjoy some me-time.

Coloring isn't just for kids! Adults can benefit from coloring, too, especially if they're stressed or anxious. Color can help you to relax and take some time out of your day to do something fun.

Coloring is a great hobby for many reasons. It can help you relax and de-stress, it's something that anyone can do regardless of age or skill level, and it's also a fun way to spend time with friends and family.

Coloring is a great way for adults to relax and destress. When we're feeling stressed or anxious, it's easy to let that affect our moods and interactions with others. Coloring can help you take some time out of your day to relax and enjoy yourself — whether you're an expert artist or just getting started on a new hobby!

Coloring can be a fun activity for the whole family. It's also an excellent way for parents to bond with their kids — whether they're coloring together or doing it separately. Coloring is an easy and inexpensive way to de-stress and destress. It will help you unwind from your day and let go of whatever is bothering you to enjoy much-needed relaxation.

Do you feel like there's never enough time for everything you have to do? Like you're always feeling stressed out? Or that you're unable to control your mood? Or struggles with anxiety and depression (or both)? If this sounds familiar, it might help to take a step back and look at the bigger picture. When you have time to relax — take a deep breath. When you feel stressed or overwhelmed, take a break. When your mind is racing, find some quiet time at the end of the day. These small steps can help reverse stress and anxiety over time.

Relaxing can be challenging, especially if you're feeling stressed or anxious. But even just taking a few deep breaths each day can help reduce feelings of stress, anxiety, and depression.

It can also help you get more sleep, which is essential for feeling relaxed and refreshed in the morning.

Find a quiet place to sit or lie down, close your eyes, and breathe slowly through your nose and out through your mouth. Use this time as an opportunity to think about anything that's bothering you or causing stress. You'll feel calmer, happier, and less stressed by relaxing for a few minutes each day.

Try to make time each day to relax and unwind. It doesn't have to be long—even just five minutes can help you feel more at ease. If you don't have time during the day, try taking a bath before bed or listening to soothing music while you do chores around the house.

Taking time to relax is essential, but it doesn't have to be complicated. Try some of these simple strategies and see what works best for you.

I find myself having an impulsive need to write words that help people. Sometimes it's just simple pieces of advice; sometimes, it's long and thoughtful reflections. Other times it's a few tips on improving your morning routine. Yet sometimes, writing can be challenging. The blank page in front of me can be daunting because I'm getting lured into anxiety instead of just finding a way to tap into my thoughts and focus on making something beautiful.

The blank page can be intimidating. It's the same feeling I get when I have a meaningful conversation with someone, and I don't know how to start talking about something on my mind. Or when I have a big test and haven't studied for it as much as I should have.

As a writer, I've learned that the blank page is an opportunity to create something beautiful. It's also a chance to improve at writing and thinking about my craft. The more I write, the easier it is for me to tap into what's going on in my head and put my thoughts down on paper.

I'm not going to lie; coloring's therapeutic effects are a significant reason I'm so into the pastime. It's also great for stress reduction and relaxation, so I'd like to share it with you!

I'm a big fan of adult coloring books. I have a few different ones and use my colored markers with them.

I enjoyed coloring as a kid, but for most of my life, it was something I occasionally did with my daughter when she was a child. It wasn't until I discovered adult coloring books that I realized just how enjoyable this simple pastime could be.

Color therapy is an ancient practice, first mentioned in a Chinese medical text 5000 years ago. It was used to treat everything from headaches to depression and is still popular today.

So, whether or not you suffer from stress-related disorders, coloring is a great way to relax and spend time doing something good for your mental health. With the increasing pace of modern life, there's room for this activity. If you want to try it, consider grabbing some coloring books and pencils and taking thirty minutes to relax with a project that will leave you feeling physically and mentally better.

Many people around the globe use color therapy, and some studies have shown its effectiveness in helping with issues like stress and anxiety. If you're feeling stressed out or anxious, give it a try. You might just find some relief from your problems.

The coloring trend shows no sign of slowing down, which is excellent. The evidence shows that coloring can help reduce stress, calm the mind, and increase creativity. These benefits have been shown to improve mental health. And overall, the research on coloring and meditation suggests that adopting simple daily rituals like these can benefit health and happiness.

At the end of the day, however, it doesn't matter if you pick up a coloring book because the pictures give you a sense of escape or because they're scientifically proven to reduce your stress levels—or some combination of both. The best part about adult coloring books is that it's entirely up to you. So whether it's color therapy or just a fun book to unwind at night, here's hoping your next coloring book encourages you to tackle a brand new project!

Chapter 13: Take Time To Laugh It Off

Laughter, in all its facets, is a powerful thing. It can relieve stress and boost the immune system, it's known to reduce pain and might spur creativity, and of course, it can just make you feel good!

Did you know that laughter is good for your health? Laughing helps increase heart rate, raise blood pressure and help send oxygen to the body and brain. Laughter can broaden your perspective on life and help you be more optimistic.

Humor is an enormous asset. It helps us endure pain, resist danger, and deal with stress. Humor lightens our burdens, revives our spirits, and makes life more bearable.

Laughter and humor are essential parts of our lives. They can provide the spark that helps us deal with stress, pain, loss, and tragedy. Laughter can also be a powerful tool for bonding with others, allowing us to form friendships and deepen relationships.

Laughter is also a great stress reliever. A good joke or funny story can take your mind off your worries and make you feel better. Humor can help us cope with difficult situations by making light of them, allowing us to see them in a new way.

I'm sure we'll have the best laugh ever, but for now, I'll keep you in suspense...

Take time to laugh. It is a potent medicine. Don't make time for it, and you'll have to make time for it later.

So, if you're not taking time to laugh every day, you should. It's good for your health.

Laughter is the best medicine. It's been shown to help us live longer and healthier and to ward off illnesses like Alzheimer's and heart disease.

I keep a list of jokes with my top picks on it. I don't tell them very often because they're not the funniest, but they make me laugh out loud.

My wife and I went to the comedy club last night, which was the best way to end a stressful day.

Some people would say they don't have time to laugh. I think they're playing with the wrong idea of what it means to laugh.

I giggled as I thought about how, quite apart from being a great laugh and a memorable guy, he'd also helped me dodge an uncomfortable moment or two with his gift for improvising comedic lines.

I've had some of my best laughs with the people I love. We shared a good laugh over how he'd been half asleep but managed to get up and find his toothbrush without bumping into anything. It was just one more example of how this guy could make anything funny.

Some people might think laughter is a waste of time. I disagree. Laughter is good for the soul, and it makes life more enjoyable. I've had some of my best laughs with the people I love. We shared a good laugh over how he'd been half asleep but managed to get up and find his toothbrush without bumping into anything. It was just one more example of how this guy could make anything funny.

If you're looking to improve your mental health, why not turn to one of the most natural stimuli: humor? Humor is a simple coping mechanism that has been around since the beginning of time, and it's something that can help you manage stress anytime—whether you're facing a busy day of projects or just trying to make it through life with a smile. So take 20 minutes out of each day for some quality laughs. Good mental health is within reach.

Sometimes, spending time with friends or family is the best way to improve your mental health. There is no better medicine than a good sense of humor. Watching a funny movie or cracking jokes with friends can be therapeutic.

If you need help with your mental health, reach out. No one is too big for the little things in life; no one is too big for laughter. But even if you don't need or want help, remember: you're not alone. You're surrounded by people who want to help. So if you need a little bit of extra love or someone to hang out with—reach out. Many people would gladly participate in a laugh, no matter where they are. And small moments of laughter can make a world of difference in someone's mood and outlook on life. So regardless of what kind of day you're having, remember that there's always room for a laugh at the end of it all.

Remember, your mental health is worth fighting for. Take care of it by exercising regularly and by, getting enough sleep, eating right, drinking in moderation, and smiling whenever you can. If you tend to your mental health, it will reward you with a host of benefits in addition to happiness and good cheer—and on those stressful days that seem never-ending, remember all the positive aspects of your life that you're lucky to have experienced.

Chapter 14: Go Off The Grid And Refresh

The best way to deal with being overwhelmed or stressed is to go off the grid literally. Leave your smartphone at home for a day and disconnect from constant emails, alerts, and other interruptions. Spend time doing something fun with someone face-to-face, which always makes you feel good.

Take a deep breath, repeat after me: "My mental health is more important than my email", and now try not to respond to this email as you browse your favorite blog. I call it the "mental health break." It's a day to go off the grid: no cell phone, landline phone, or computer. Don't even check your voicemail. All you do all day is enjoy the company of those you love and do what's fun for you.

When you have depression, it's easy to become imprisoned by feelings that drag you down. Do something different. Get up and get out of the house. Find something fun to do with someone you like. The emotional boost will help you get through this low period. You don't realize how meaningful those connections are until you temporarily lose them.

Did you know that people who spend more time on their mobile devices or smartphones are less happy and less healthy? It's true! Spending too much time working in front of a screen or looking at electronic devices can negatively impact your mental health. Studies have suggested that these devices keep us from having true face-to-face conversations with each other. This is a loss for everyone.

We are constantly connected. We have smartphones, tablets, and many other digital devices that always need our attention. Before you know it, you're snapping at the people around you because they're not responding to your text messages fast enough. That's why it's essential to recognize the stress we place on ourselves and how we could benefit from doing less.

One of my clients, a startup COO, told me, 'If we can just get them to stop emailing us so much, everything would be easier.' And she was right! Email is pervasive and makes even the simplest task grind to a halt. We're so bombarded with emails that it becomes tempting to answer and read emails that aren't important. Developing new ways to manage your inbox can help you achieve more.

I went off the grid. My cell phone stayed at home. For the first time in years, I didn't use email or any other online accounts for an entire day.

I went out with friends and family, and I enjoyed it. I still had my laptop and could do work if I wanted to, but I didn't need to check my email or get caught up on social media posts. If you stay off the grid for an entire day, you'll better understand how much time you waste checking your devices.

I did a brain dump. In my journal, I wrote everything I was feeling, thinking, and worrying about. Writing these down helped me organize my thoughts; when I looked back at them later, they didn't seem so overwhelming anymore.

I meditated. I've never been big on meditation, but it benefited me in this situation. It helped me focus my thoughts and calm down, so I wasn't worrying about something that'd happened hours ago or stressing about what would happen the following week.

I took a walk. It was amazing how much better I felt after getting some fresh air and stretching my legs. I also enjoyed looking at the leaves on the trees and thinking about how they change colors in the fall.

I played with a pet. My dog is my best friend, and it was nice to spend some time with him. He's always happy to see me when I get home from work, so we played fetch for a while and then watched TV together on the couch.

I took a shower. It's incredible how much better I feel after taking a hot shower, especially if I've been feeling stressed or overwhelmed by work. It helps me relax and unwind and makes me feel clean and refreshed!

I ate a snack. I had some leftover pizza in the fridge, so I heated it on my way home from work and ate it while watching TV with my dog. It was a delicious way to end my day!

The simple fact is that there are clear mental health benefits for those who go off the grid regularly. Try it for even a day, and you may be surprised at how easy it is to return to your old habits afterward.

When we put things off or never take the time to plan something fun, this leaves us feeling like those tasks will never get done. Spending time doing something positive and fulfilling will improve your mental health, leaving you more hopeful about tackling more significant problems later.

It can be hard to improve mental health when you're so busy that it's all you can do to survive the week or even the day. It would be easy for me to give you a simple solution like "Get outside." But improving your mental health is more complex than that. It requires a variety of things: increasing self-awareness, starting a new hobby, regular exercise, and diet—it's not something you can achieve quickly in one or two steps. I recommend making minor changes to your everyday routine and enjoying life as much as possible on the way.

The critical thing to remember is that it's challenging to maintain a positive mental and physical state if you don't first take care of yourself. Take the time to put your health first. If you manage this, the rest will follow. And then you'll be able to enjoy all the good things that life has in store for you.

The bottom line is that you have to care and improve yourself. Do what's right for you, just like Matt did, because life is too short not to try everything you can. Since writing this article, I've taken a step back and let several things go. I now consume much less news on Twitter and find other means of engaging with people.

As more smartphone and mobile technologies become available, it is essential that we work towards maintaining a healthy balance between work and social activities. We may not be able to stop the evolution of technology, but we can at least take the time to monitor our digital habits. Dealing with stress through social interactions and face-to-face meetings will only help us benefit more from new technology. It's easy to get caught up in the "stress of perfection" and lose sight of what brought us to this job in the first place: to create.

Chapter 15: House Dance

I've recently become interested in mental health (specifically, as it relates to personality type), and have been spending a lot of time reading about it. I first discovered that a very common way to improve your mental health is to start doing your chores while dancing.

Housework is so boring, and too many dread doing it. But I stumbled across a site that said to dance while you do it, and help gets done faster, with less dawdling. I was incredulous but tried it anyway.

The best cure for what ails you is often as simple as taking a walk or dancing around your living room. And, if not that, then there is always medication. But unless you are in crisis, your doctor will probably prescribe exercise, meditation, counseling, or talking with a friend. This counseling or talking with a friend can be done one-on-one or in a self-help group.

Housework is better with music, and so is mental health. But why?

Being happier is something to strive for, not just in our work and personal lives but also in ourselves. Anyone can improve their mental health with some simple lifestyle choices: eat better, get more exercise, and sleep more, all the while being mindful of their emotions. And it doesn't take a doctor—just a little research and determination.

Life is difficult for many people. Life is full of difficult problems. Of those difficult problems, many are personal and can probably be solved by a little introspection.

Dancing while you do your chores is a great way to have fun, get your chores done, and help your health!

I'll wrap up this chapter by saying that I'm not trying to tell you to dance while you do your chores. I don't have any studies to back me up with this. But I think it's a good idea, and I will try it.

The next time you do tedious chores around the house, put on your favorite music and dance.

So the next time you're vacuuming your living room, put on some music and dance like nobody's watching.

I learned that dancing around while doing chores isn't just a crazy idea I had. It makes sense when you think about it.

The next time you find yourself at loose ends, try a little dance therapy.

I'm sure you could find a way to dance around without looking like a crazy person, and I bet you'd feel better about it.

I have a confession to make. I'm a compulsive cleaner, and I like to dance.

I don't know about you, but I find it impossible to dance and clean in the same room.

I knew I had to do something drastic. Because on a day-to-day basis, I was too busy and exhausted to get any real exercise.

That's why they invented dance.

I'm not talking about going to a dance class or anything. I mean dancing around your living room while vacuuming, dusting, and doing the laundry. It's quite easy once you get the hang of it. Just put on some music that makes you feel good (I like salsa) and start moving your hips around in time to the beat.

You'll be surprised at how much energy you get from dancing. And the best part is that it's fun! So why not try it? It might just change your life.

If you're not sure what kind of music to put on, try listening to some salsa or merengue. And remember, it doesn't have to be fancy dancing; just moving your hips in time with the beat will do. If you like dancing, consider joining a salsa class or taking lessons from an instructor (I've found that instructors tend to emphasize technique more than enjoyment).

If you don't like dancing, try it anyway! You may find that you enjoy it.

Dancing is a great workout. But more importantly, it's fun! It certainly beats cleaning the house while being bored. So, the next time you have a daunting chore, put on some good music and start dancing while you do it. You'll find that the time will pass quicker than you think, and you'll enjoy it too.

I've been dancing around the house every day for about three years. I highly recommend it; it makes chores much more fun (I love to say "dance as you clean"), and I've also enjoyed the other physiological benefits. Give it a try, and let me know how it goes!

Most of us know that dancing is fun and will leave you smiling. But did you know that regular dancing can also provide excellent health benefits? Dancing has been linked to stress reduction, better sleep, weight loss, increased energy, lower blood pressure, improved immune function, and reduced anxiety levels. And if you're looking for a way to lose weight or improve your fitness level (while having fun), dancing is an excellent physical activity with family or friends. Even better, studies have shown that doing housework while listening to music positively impacts motivation and performance. Have fun while you clean!

Instead of feeling frustrated about having to mop, vacuum, or clean your bathroom, why not make a game out of it? Feel free to cartwheels and handstands across the kitchen while cleaning dinner. Dance like nobody's watching. Or are they?

Now it's time to get up off the floor and go back to work.

Conclusion

This book has covered all tips for improving your mental health to help you achieve a happier, healthier lifestyle. I sincerely hope these tips help you live a better life and feel more confident in taking on all the day-to-day challenges you will inevitably face.

Eating well, getting regular exercise, and getting adequate sleep are the cornerstones of good mental health, but there are plenty of other ways to keep your mind healthy. We've compiled a list of tips that will help you feel better both physically and mentally, and we hope they will help you live happier and more fulfilling lives.

Treat your mental health like anything else in life, and do your best to take care of yourself. Our lives become hectic practically at the drop of a hat, with each day becoming more stressful than the last. It's crucial that we find ways to relieve stress, whether it's through a hobby, exercise, or out-of-the-box methods. We may never be perfect in our efforts to stay happy and healthy mentally, but we can always do better.

Improving your mental health is a complex and challenging process to change. It takes hard work, time, and effort, but the first steps are making small changes such as eating healthier, sleeping well, exercising more, and so forth. Once you have gotten into a good routine over a few days, weeks, or months, you should find a counselor or therapist to help you along the way.

Above all, remember to take it easy on yourself. It's understandable if you experience a few frustrating days or weeks at the beginning of your journey toward improving your mental health. Just be sure not to lose sight of the ultimate goal and how far you've already come. And when you find that things aren't going as smoothly as you had hoped, it can help remind you that something might have been even worse if you hadn't started in the first place.

So, as you can see, there are many reasons to improve your mental health. And it's never too late to begin making positive changes in your life.

If you're ready to take the first step toward improving your mental health, many resources are available to help you get started. Talk with a supportive friend or family member, or contact a professional counselor at your local community center. You can also check out some of the resources provided in this book for more information on different types of therapy and other ways to improve your mental health.

In addition to working on your mental health, getting enough sleep and exercise is also important. Both of these activities can reduce stress levels and boost your mood.

Contact your local emergency services if you're in crisis and need help immediately. They can provide immediate assistance if you're feeling suicidal or having another mental health crisis. If you don't know where to find these services, ask a friend or family member for help or call 911.

If you need more help than what's covered in this book, consider contacting a mental health professional. You may want to start with a therapist or psychiatrist.

You can find out if your health insurance covers mental health care by checking with them or looking at their website.

If you don't have insurance, there are other options to consider. For example, many states offer mental health services through community health centers. You can also contact your local hospital or university medical center and ask them what resources they provide.

Several free or low-cost mental health resources are available if you don't have any of these options. For example, SAMHSA has a directory of local mental health programs and facilities. You can also use their online screening tool to find out if you have a mental health problem and get advice on what to do next.

If you have insurance, it's a good idea to contact your insurer and ask about mental health benefits. You may be able to get help from them or a specific mental health provider in their network. If not, you can also check out SAMHSA's directory of providers for low-cost or free care.

The key takeaway is that everyone needs a little self-care. As we just read, and yes, you know it is on your mind, it's chocolate, but you can find other ways to help yourself feel better throughout your day as well. Make sure to schedule some "me time" to relax and do something you enjoy every now and then. Go on walks. Read books. Listen to music. Meet with friends or family members. Whatever it is, take whatever time is necessary to make yourself feel good—that feeling of well-being will come through in your work more so than you might think!

Don't miss out!

Visit the website below and you can sign up to receive emails whenever Adam Smith publishes a new book. There's no charge and no obligation.

https://books2read.com/r/B-A-OSAW-NWLDC

Connecting independent readers to independent writers.

Also by Adam Smith

The Hidden Communication Tool: Why Businesses Need A Blog
Brain Dead: When It Comes To Improving Mental Health, What The Hell Are We Waiting For?

Watch for more at https://asmith.media.

About the Author

Adam Smith is a native North Texas Entrepreneur, social media expert, and educator who graduated from Embry Riddle University with a Bachelor of Science in Aerospace Studies. In 2007 he co-founded TeacherTube.com, an online education platform community that provides educationally focused, safe venue for teachers, schools, and home learners. Under his leadership in September of 2017, publicly traded company, Salem Media Group, acquired TeacherTube. At the time of acquisition, TeacherTube had over 2 million registered educators with over 12 million monthly unique views to the site.

After the acquisition, Adam continued his passion for technology and education by helping schools and start-ups to large corporations with online training, branding, content marketing and social media management.

Find out more about Adam, go to https://asmith.media or http://adamsmithspeaks.com.

Read more at https://asmith.media.

About the Publisher

A. Smith Media is a fully integrated digital media and distribution company specializing in producing and marketing television, film, home entertainment, music, and interactive games. A. Smith Media has been at the forefront of the commercial growth of Digital Distribution and Internet Video on Demand services through its pioneering efforts in web TV.

www.ingramcontent.com/pod-product-compliance
Lightning Source LLC
LaVergne TN
LVHW090333210926
848480LV00004B/1393
* 9 7 9 8 2 1 5 1 5 7 3 8 1 *